US edition © 2024 by Amy Jones
Published by Wooden Books LLC,
San Rafael, California

First published in the UK in 2022
by Wooden Books Ltd, Glastonbury, UK

Library of Congress Cataloging-in-Publication Data
Jones, A.
Narrative

Library of Congress Cataloging-in-Publication
Data has been applied for

ISBN-10: 1-952178-36-3
ISBN-13: 978-1-952178-36-8

Designed and typeset in Glastonbury, UK

Printed in China on FSC® certified papers by
RR Donnelley Asia Printing Solutions Ltd.

NARRATIVE
TELLING THE STORY

Amy Jones

for my parents

Recommend further reading: *Exercises in Style*, Raymond Queneau; *Narrative Discourse*, Gerard Genette; *The Science of Storytelling*, Will Storr; *Story and Discourse: Narrative Structure in Fiction and Film*, Seymour Chatman; *Between the Lines: Master the Subtle Elements of Fiction Writing*, Jessica Page Morrell; *Dialogue: The Art of Verbal Action for Page, Stage, and Screen*, Robert McKee.

THE THEORY OF NARRATOLOGY

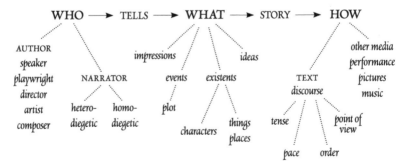

ABOVE: **NARRATOLOGY**, *the science of narration, can be simplified as one simple question:* **WHO TELLS WHAT HOW?** — *as illustrated in the diagram above (after Manfred Jahn, A Guide to the Theory of Narrative, University of Cologne, 2021).*

INTRODUCTION

IT IS ONE THING to plot a story. Telling it is another matter. This book covers narrative method, the art of turning a plot into a tale well told. In the pages which follow, we will explore the fascinating range of narrative methods which have been developed and wielded over the centuries by some of the world's finest storytellers. On every page in every chapter, an author must select the best way to relate the scene, carefully choosing the viewpoint and focus that will suit their purpose and pull their readers, listeners and viewers into the characters and the world of their story.

While this book deals with the telling of a story, the art of constructing and refining a story and plot is covered in our sister book: *Plot: The Art of Story*. You may want to read that alongside this.

Fashions in narrative come and go. Most early novels, such as Henry Fielding's *Tom Jones* (1749), were written from the perspective of a third person, whereas nineteenth century authors, such as Mary Shelley, in *Frankenstein* (1818), and Charlotte Brontë, in *Jane Eyre* (1847), drew readers closer to their characters using private letters and first person viewpoints. In the early 20th century, writers such as James Joyce and Virginia Woolf brought readers even closer, penning the unfiltered stream-of-consciousness of their protagonists.

Narrative viewpoints have evolved too, with authors increasingly telling stories from the points of view of children, women, animals, plants, villains, and even aliens, alongside those of adult male heroes.

Crucial decisions around your narrative style will ultimately characterise your work. As Jack Kerouac [1922–1969] famously wrote:

> It ain't whatcha write, it's the way atcha write it.

THE NARRATIVE SITUATION

one or many

***

THIS LITTLE BOOK takes you through five key choices that a writer needs to make when it comes to delivering their tale:

1. WHO WILL TELL THE STORY?

* * *Who is the NARRATOR?*
* * *Are they REMOTE, or involved as a CHARACTER in the story?*
* * *What is their NARRATIVE VOICE?*
* * *Is there ONE narrator, or are there MULTIPLE narrators?*

2. WHO WILL SEE THE STORY?

* * *Who is the FOCALISER: Who are we following?*
* * *How close to their thoughts and actions are we: What is the DISTANCE?*
* * *Is there one focaliser, or two, three, or more MULTIPLE focalisers?*

3. WHEN IS THE STORY TOLD?

* * *What is the TENSE? Is the story set in the past, present or future?*
* * *Does the book employ MULTIPLE tenses?*
* * *What is the ORDER of events: Chronological, or do we jump around?*
* * *What SPEED does the story go?*

4. HOW IS THE STORY TOLD?

* * *Is the story told straight up, or framed within another story?*
* * *Does the book employ any other narrative devices?*

5. WHAT MODE IS USED TO TELL THE STORY?

* * *Will the story be told with a balance of modes, or will one prevail?*
* * *In what mode will the story start?*

These core components of the storyteller's art meld into the unified **NARRATIVE SITUATION**. This is what characterises a work, at any given moment in a book, and right from the first page. A single work may contain a variety of narrative situations, including a range of first person narrators, or a mixture of first and third person styles. It may use ephemera, like diary entries and letters. It may jump around in time or flip the tense. It may use multiple focalisers, as the existing narrative situation gives way to allow another character to take the viewpoint.

A well-crafted narrative situation will keep the audience interested, the characters interesting, and the story moving. Events which might normally appear absurd or out of the ordinary will flow naturally, while the common-place will be taken for granted (we will assume that characters go to bed and wake up every day without being told that they do).

Each narrative approach has a unique effect. The choice depends on what the author seeks to achieve in terms of the tone of the work, the character development, pace, suspense and other factors. If you are a budding writer, you should experiment with multiple narrative forms until you find those which most naturally fit your personal style.

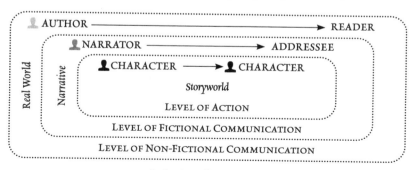

ABOVE: *The three levels of narrative communication*

3

WHO TELLS THE STORY?
the narrator

In ancient times, storytelling required a storyteller, and today, in every work of fiction, sandwiched between the author and the reader/listener/viewer, there exists a **NARRATOR**, overt or covert, who, in their own special **NARRATIVE VOICE**, relays the **NARRATIVE** to the **NARRATEE**—the *imagined* person whom the narrator assumes they are addressing.

> *One way you can think of the narrator is almost as a kind of character, an implicit and invisible character who shapes, filters, orders and presents the narrative information that we have access to.*   Michael Filimowicz

There are various kinds of narrators. They are either outside the action or part of it. There is either just one narrator in a book, or there are two or more (*see diagram opposite*). There are, however, three essential types:

HETERODIEGETIC: *the narrator is not an active character, but knows the story.*
HOMODIEGETIC: *the narrator is a character in the story.*
AUTODIEGETIC: *the narrator is the active protagonist.*

At the opening to the 1813 novel *Pride and Prejudice*, our heterodiegetic narrator and narratee are immediately positioned in time, place, and class:

> *It is a truth universally acknowledged that a single man in possession of a good fortune must be in want of a wife.*   Jane Austen, *Pride and Pejudice*, 1813

We are straight away Regency gossips, intimate equals of narrator Elizabeth Bennet, propelled into the lives of the novel's characters. This fictional space is sometimes called the **STORYWORLD,** a term coined by cognitive narratologist David Herman to describe both the specific narrative and the entire imagined reality constructed by the narrator.

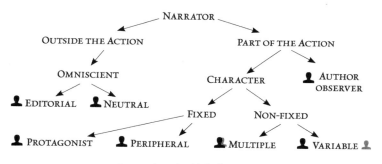

ABOVE: *The various kinds of narrators.*

The writer puts on the skin of the narrator to present their interpretation of events, like an actor playing a role for stage or film. The narrative voice needs to be that of a convincing individual whose idiosyncrasies—personal biases, flaws, values, intelligence, regional dialect, etc.—we recognise as part of their nature, whether they are removed from the action, as here, in Dicken's heterodiegetic narration:

> *External heat and cold had little influence on Scrooge. No warmth could warm, no wintry weather chill him. No wind that blew was bitterer than he, no falling snow was more intent upon its purpose, no pelting rain less open to entreaty. Foul weather didn't know where to have him. The heaviest rain, and snow, and hail, and sleet, could boast of the advantage over him in only one respect. They often "came down" handsomely, and Scrooge never did.* Charles Dickens, A Christmas Carol, 1843

or part of it, with an extremely modified voice, close to spoken word, a style known as *skaz*, as here, in Twain's autodiegetic narrative:

> *… if I'd a knowed what a trouble it was to make a book I wouldn't a tackled it, and ain't a-going to no more. But I reckon I got to light out for the Territory ahead of the rest, because Aunt Sally she's going to adopt me and sivilize me, and I can't stand it.* Mark Twain, Huckleberry Finn, 1884

THIRD-PERSON OMNISCIENT
our story begins

THIRD-PERSON OMNISCIENT is arguably the original narrative voice in written English. In this time-tested mode the heterodiegetic narrator is entirely removed from the action, and uses third person pronouns, such as *he*, *she*, *her*, *his*, *they* and *their*, to describe the unfolding story. The technique is found in early texts such as the c. 6th century Old English epic *Beowulf*:

> So lived the clansmen in cheer and revel | a winsome life, till one began | to fashion evils, that field of hell. | Grendel this monster grim was called, | march-riever mighty, in moorland living, | in fen and fastness; fief of the giants | the hapless wight a while had kept | since the Creator his exile doomed.

through to Tolstoy's 1869 magnum opus, *War and Peace*:

> Just then another visitor entered the drawing room: Prince Andrew Bolkónski, the little princess' husband. He was a very handsome young man, of medium height, with firm, clearcut features. Everything about him, from his weary, bored expression to his quiet, measured step, offered a most striking contrast to his quiet, little wife.

With a god-like perspective, an omniscient narrator can skip from character to character, in and out of their eyes, hearts and minds, across rooms, countries, chapters and episodes, following incidents in the plot, commenting on things, and all the time gently drawing the reader along, either with a neutral voice or a personal engaging style. Here is an extract from *Vanity Fair*, written by William Makepeace Thackeray in 1848:

> Amelia meanwhile, in Russell Square, was looking at the moon, which was shining upon that peaceful spot, as well as upon the square of the Chatham barracks, where Lieutenant Osborne was quartered, and thinking to herself how her hero was employed. Perhaps he is visiting the sentries, thought she; perhaps he is bivouacking; perhaps he

is attending the couch of a wounded comrade, or studying the art of war up in his own desolate chamber. And her kind thoughts sped away as if they were angels and had wings, and flying down the river to Chatham and Rochester, strove to peep into the barracks where George was … All things considered, I think it was well the gates were shut, and the sentry allowed no one to pass; so that the poor little white-robed angel could not hear the songs those young fellows were roaring over the whiskey punch.

Omniscient POV was the choice of most 19th century writers, ideal for subplots, intrigues and DRAMATIC IRONY (where the full significance of a character's words or actions is clear to us, but not to them). Today, with its ever-moving authorial perspective, it is mostly out of fashion.

A cousin of third-person omniscient is THIRD-PERSON OBJECTIVE. Here the narrator stays distant, and has no access to characters' thoughts or feelings. Ernest Hemingway uses it to punchy effect in a short story, written in 1927:

The American and the girl with him sat at a table in the shade, outside the building. It was very hot and the express from Barcelona would come in forty minutes. It stopped at this junction for two minutes and went on to Madrid.

"What should we drink?" the girl asked. She had taken off her hat and put it on the table.

"It's pretty hot," the man said. "Let's drink beer."

"Dos cervezas," the man said into the curtain.

"Big ones?" a woman asked from the doorway.

"Yes. Two big ones."

Ernest Hemingway, *Hills Like White Elephants*, 1927

THIRD-PERSON FOCALISED
this is their experience

A **THIRD-PERSON FOCALISED** narrative (also known as **CLOSE THIRD**) tells the story as experienced by a single character. We share the thought patterns, character and responses of this individual, connecting us much more closely to them than in the roving omniscient mode. Author Ursula Le Guin provides a helpful overview:

> Only what the viewpoint character knows, feels, perceives, thinks, guesses, hopes, remembers, etc., can be told. The reader can infer what other people feel only from what the viewpoint character observes of their behaviour... *Steering the Craft*, 1998

All seven of J.K. Rowling's *Harry Potter* novels are written in close third. Every scene is written from the **POINT OF VIEW** (**POV**) of our eponymous hero:

> "Up!" she screeched. Harry heard her walking toward the kitchen and then the sound of the frying pan being put on the stove. He rolled onto his back and tried to remember the dream he had been having. It had been a good one. There had been a flying motorcycle in it. He had a funny feeling he'd had the same dream before.
>
> *Harry Potter and the Philosopher's Stone*, Ch.2 The-Vanishing-Glass, 2001

Hilary Mantel's award-winning 2010 novel *Wolf Hall* is focalised throughout by its lead character Thomas Cromwell. It opens *in media res*:

> PUTNEY, 1500. "So now get up."
> Felled, dazed, silent, he has fallen; knocked full length on the cobbles of the yard. His head turns sideways; his eyes are turned toward the gate, as if someone might arrive to help him out. One blow, properly placed, could kill him now.

A **THIRD-PERSON MULTIPLE** narrative focalises through two or more characters. Examples include *Anna Karenina*, *Madame Bovary*, and *Bonfire of* *the Vanities*. In his 1996 bestseller *A Game of Thrones*, George R.R. Martin focalises his story through the eyes of eight characters, with each of the 72 chapters switching viewpoint between them (*see chapter list above*).

Focalised third allows readers to be kept in the dark about threats and twists that the character is unaware of, building tension. Writers can zoom in and out of character viewpoints, allowing insightful character development alongside third-person objectivity which moves the plot along. It can, however, limit the development of other characters.

Here are some tips for this popular method: Choose your focaliser(s) carefully—they may not be the obvious choice. Don't use words and sayings that your character would never use. Allow your individual to make guesses and build connection and suspense with the reader. Be aware of your DISTANCE from them (*see page 24*): are you in their head, behind it, or slightly further away? Keep your narrative voice small and neutral, like a reporter. Show, don't tell: instead of She was amazed, try Her eyes widened; she smiled and shook her head. Oh, and don't head-hop mid scene!

First-Person Peripheral
I saw it all, let me tell you

In **FIRST-PERSON PERIPHERAL** narration, events are recounted by an ancillary character who witnesses the protagonist's story. The most famous example is Nick Carraway in F. Scott Fitzgerald's 1925 novel *The Great Gatsby.* In 1920s America our narrator watches agape as glamorous, wealthy and morally corrupt characters float about him. At times defensive and unreliable, Nick is himself a writer, giving creative flair to his voice:

> *I'm inclined to reserve all judgments... for the intimate revelations of young men, or at least the terms in which they express them, are usually plagiaristic and marred by obvious suppressions. Reserving judgments is a matter of infinite hope.*

Fitzgerald also focalises from Gatsby's point of view:

> *His heart beat faster as Daisy's white face came up to his own. He knew that when he kissed this girl... his mind would never romp again like the mind of God. So he waited...*

although Carraway's own first-person narrative is ever-present:

> *Through all he said, even through his appalling sentimentality, I was reminded of something — an elusive rhythm, a fragment of lost words, that I had heard somewhere a long time ago.*

In Aphra Behn's 1688 short novel *Oroonoko*, the narrator is an unnamed Englishwoman who positions herself on the periphery right from the start:

> *I was my self an Eye-Witness to a great part, of what you will find here set down; and what I cou'd not be Witness of, I receiv'd from the Mouth of the chief Actor in this History, the Hero himself.*

Peripheral narrators part a play in the story and are often self conscious of this in the telling, adding an intriguing layer to a narrative. In the examples just given, both narrators are ostensibly writing to commemorate the death of a friend—an impossible perspective in close third or first person central narratives, whose narrators cannot survive their own death. However, we may also infer that they are motivated to exonerate themselves, so we question their agendas and reliability (*see pages 24–27*).

By contrast, in the *Sherlock Holmes* stories, Dr Watson acts as a highly trustworthy intermediary between ourselves and the exceptional but difficult detective, relaying all of Holmes' extraordinary adventures to us in his own calm manner. Here, they meet for the very first time:

> *"Dr. Watson, Mr. Sherlock Holmes," said Stamford, introducing us.*
> *"How are you?" he said cordially, gripping my hand with a strength for which I should hardly have given him credit. "You have been in Afghanistan, I perceive."*
> *"How on earth did you know that?" I asked in astonishment.*
> *"Never mind," said he, chuckling to himself.* Arthur Conan Doyle, A Study in Scarlet, 1887

First-person peripheral allows for a more secretive and mysterious protagonist. This, combined with the ability of the narrator to make their own observations on matters, including on the character of the protagonist, can cast interesting light and shadows into the subtle worlds of this complex narrative method.

FIRST-PERSON CENTRAL
my story is about me

We have, at last, arrived at the most intimate of all narrative methods, **FIRST-PERSON CENTRAL** (or **FIRST-PERSON POV**), a story written from the personal point of view of the protagonist, who finally *becomes* the narrator. Calling themselves "I", they relay their story to us directly:

> *I cast my Eyes to the stranded Vessel, when the Breach and Froth of the Sea being so big, I could hardly see it, it lay so far off, and considered, Lord! how was it possible I could get on Shore?* Daniel Defoe, Robinson Crusoe, 1719

Done well, with careful planning and research, a first-person narrative voice can draw us directly into a world far removed from our own, as we focalise exclusively through someone else's eyes and mind. References to the past, as well as the present, help build a convincing storyworld:

> *My name is Kathy H. I'm thirty-one years old, and I've been a carer now for over eleven years. That sounds long enough, I know, but actually they want me to go on for another eight months, until the end of this year. That'll make it almost exactly twelve years.* Kazuo Ishiguro, Never Let Me Go, 2005

The close and immersive nature nature of first-person POV allows the reader to experience events at the same time as the main character, enabling an acute sense of pace and drama. It is ideal for thrillers. Here, Suzanne Collins captures the emotion of the inciting incident for her entire trilogy:

> *…I reach her just as she is about to mount the steps. With one sweep of my arm, I push her behind me. "I volunteer!" I gasp. "I volunteer as tribute!"* The Hunger Games, 2008

When writing in this style, use early on to reveal actions and confidences that make the reader care, but create suspense by retaining other secrets for later. Avoid distancing filter words like I saw, I heard etc., and passive phrases like The ball was kicked by me. Do not assume omniscient knowledge of other characters: instead of I gave Jane the key; she was delighted try As I passed Jane the key, her face lit up. Only write what you see/hear/smell/taste/feel.

There is a seldom-used **FIRST-PERSON OMNISCIENT** mode. Here the first-person narrator *can* access the thoughts, actions and motivations of other characters. In Markus Zusak's 2005 bestseller *The Book Thief*, the first-person omniscient narrator turns out to be truly omniscient. Similarly, Lemony Snicket, the author and first-person narrator in *A Series of Unfortunate Events* has almost god-like access to all his characters.

Writers increasingly use **MULTIPLE FIRST-PERSON** viewpoints. In her best-selling 2012 thriller *Gone Girl*, author Gillian Flynn alternates chapters between the first person accounts of Nick Dunne and Amy Elliott, who each take turns to tell their version of events and fight for our trust, as we gradually realise that one of them must be lying to us:

> When I think of my wife, I always think of her head. The shape of it, to begin with. The very first time I saw her, it was the back of the head I saw, and there was something lovely about it, the angles of it. Nick. Start of Chapter 1

> I am fat with love! Husky with ardor! Morbidly obese with devotion! A happy, busy bumblebee of marital enthusiasm. I positively hum around him, fussing and fixing. I have become a strange thing. I have become a wife. Amy. Start of Chapter 4

STREAM OF CONSCIOUSNESS
left right up down centre

Try writing down every thought that crosses your mind in the first ten minutes after waking. Your consciousness will flit between all kinds of topics, maybe from dreams you just had, to the hopes and fears of the day ahead, from memories, bitter and sweet, to a conversation, or the sound of birdsong. **STREAM OF CONSCIOUSNESS** writing tries to emulate this chaotic flow, and its use was pioneered by modernist writers in the early 20th century. Readers may get lost in such disorderly and meandering narratives, but the style can be deeply immersive. Here is Leopold Bloom going about his day in Dublin:

> *Mr Bloom, champing, standing, looked upon his sigh. Nosey numbskull. Will I tell him that horse Lenehan? He knows already. Better let him forget. Go and lose more. Fool and his money. Dewdrop coming down again.* James Joyce, Ulysses, 1922

William Faulkner, Virginia Woolf and T.S Eliot all used this form. Toni Morrison is a contemporary adherent:

> *I am alone I want to be the two of us I want the join I come out of blue water after the bottoms of my feet swim away from me I come up I need to find a place to be the air is heavy I am not dead I am not there is a house there is what she whispered to me ...* Tony Morrison, Beloved, 1987

IT'S A STREAM OF CONSCIOUSNESS NOVEL LIKE 'ULYSSES' I JUST SORT OF SAT DOWN AND WROTE IT WITHOUT EVEN THINKING OF A PLOT HAVE YOU HAD A DRINK I'M GOING TO GET A SEAT WHERE DO YOU COME FROM IT'S HOT IN HERE I LIKE BLUE DO YOU LIKE BLUE...

SECOND-PERSON

this is about you

SECOND-PERSON narration directly addresses the reader, 'you'. Common in manuals: *Open your calendar*; recipes: *If you don't have any garlic*; and advertising; *Your country needs YOU* [1914 British recruitment poster]; it is rare in literature.

It is not hard to see why. Projecting creative, nuanced descriptions in second-person can be extremely clumsy and challenging to maintain over a long narrative. The eye of the text firmly fixes itself on the reader, as an active participant in the story, and this can be disorientating—disturbing even. However, sometimes this level of guided intimacy is precisely the effect that the author is looking for:

> You are not the kind of guy who would be at a place like this at this time of the morning. But here you are, and you cannot say that the terrain is entirely unfamiliar, although the details are fuzzy. You are at a nightclub talking to a girl with a shaved head. The club is either Heartbreak or the Lizard Lounge. All might come clear if you could just slip into the bathroom and do a little more Bolivian Marching Powder. Then again it might not. Jay McInerney, Bright Lights, Big City, 1984

This deeply immersive narrative mode has found a niche in INTERACTIVE FICTIONS, in print (e.g. Edward Packard's *Choose Your Own Adventure* series), gaming, and new electronic literature forms, as here:

> You are Primo Varicella, Palace Minister at the Palazzo del Piemonte. This title is unlikely to impress anyone. Piedmont is the laughingstock of the Carolingian League, and the Palace Ministry has devolved into little more than a glorified (and not even especially glorified) butlership: your duties include organizing banquets, overseeing the servants, and greeting visitors. It is safe to assume that the War Minister and the Coffers Minister lose little sleep over your presence in the King's Cabinet.

Adam Cadre, *Varicella*, 1999

UNRELIABLE NARRATORS
picaros and clowns

We all like to tell stories which show us in a good light. The notion of an unreliable narrator seems to have been coined by Wayne C. Booth in his 1961 work *The Rhetoric of Fiction*. Usually limited to first-person narrative, Booth considers an unreliable narrator to be one who:

> ... tells lies, conceals information, misjudges with respect to the narrative audience – that is, one whose statements are untrue not by the standards of the real world or of the authorial audience but by the standards of his own narrative audience. ... In other words, all fictional narrators are false in that they are imitations. But some are imitations who tell the truth, some of people who lie. Peter J. Rabinowitz, Truth in Fiction, 1977

Such unreliability offers readers extra layers of intrigue and realism. William Riggan identifies four types of unreliable narrator:

1. **PICARO.** *Characterised by exaggerration and bragging (below).*
2. **CLOWN.** *Takes nothing seriously and plays with conventions (opposite).*
3. **MADMAN.** *Has mental health issues, from anxiety to schizophrenia (page 18).*
4. **NAIF.** *Immature or limited in some other way (page 19).*

PICARO narrators are named after the popular Spanish picaresque dramas of the late 16th century. They have a tendency to brag and exaggerate. In Daniel Defoe's 1722 fictional autobiography *Moll Flanders*, Moll, awaiting death in a prison cell, recounts various incidents in her life with dubious aplomb. Here she frames a boy after failing to steal a watch:

> ... I had full hold of her Watch, but giving a great Jostle, as if some body had thrust me against her, and in the Juncture giving the Watch a fair pull, I found it would not come, so I let it go that Moment, and cried out as if I had been kill'd ...

Moll's subsequent narrative includes bigamy, incest, prostitution and theft. We are left empathetic for her plight, but also aware that we might be victim to a strongly self-sympathising and aggrandizing version of events, having seen her work just this kind of magic in her very own tales!

George McDonald Fraser's well-honed character Flashman frequently takes blithe braggadocio to extreme lengths in his eponymous parody of British colonial adventure:

ABOVE: Moll Flanders, by Reginald Marsh.

> *So there you have M. Henri Stefan Oppert-Blowitz, and if I've told you a deal about him and his crackpot notions of our "shared destiny," it's because they were at the root of the whole crazy business, and dam' near cost me my life, as well as preventing a great European war ...*
>
> George McDonald Fraser, *Flashman and the Tiger*, 1999

CLOWN narrators refuse to take their role seriously. They toy with our expectations as readers, lying to us for the sake of their own entertainment, and defying conventional narrative structures. *Tristram Shandy*'s narrative (*see page 33*) includes blacked out pages, censored words left for us to fill in, lengthy digressions, sketches, and further disorienting comments:

> *I have a strong propensity in me to begin this chapter very nonsensically, and I will not balk my fancy. Accordingly I set off thus...* Laurence Stern, *Tristram Shandy*, 1760s

Sometimes irritating, a whimsical and unpredictable narrator may also characterise the whole tone of a text as playful and compelling.

MORE UNRELIABLE NARRATORS
madmen and naifs

A **MADMAN** is a narrator who is unreliable due to some kind of cognitive difference, which makes them unable or unwilling to accurately interpret and relay events. They are often used in crime or mystery writing, or where an author needs to explore issues around violence, trauma or addiction. In Edgar Allen Poe's 1843 short story *The Tell Tale Heart* the narrator tells us:

> Now this is the point. You fancy me mad. Madmen know nothing. But you should have seen me. You should have seen how wisely I proceeded - with what caution - with what foresight - with what dissimulation I went to work! I was never kinder to the old man than during the whole week before I killed him.

The immediacy of this narrative voice, the pauses and repetition, all contribute to the sense that we are listening to the confession of a man who has crossed over into insanity. Poe is the master of creating this kind of claustrophobia; the reader feels trapped in a room with a self-confessed murderer. Similarly, Patrick Bateman, narrator in *American Psycho*, admits to a perception of reality that renders it unreliable:

> I had all the characteristics of a human being — flesh, blood, skin, hair — but my depersonalization was so intense, had gone so deep, that my normal ability to feel compassion had been eradicated ... Bret Easton Ellis, *American Psycho*, 1991

A **NAIF** is an unreliable narrator because of their naivety—they tell us their impressions and experiences, but it is up to the reader to see through it all and understand what is really going on. Their naivety comes from a lack of understanding or control of the world around them:

> ... I left all the foils and equipment and stuff on the goddam subway ... The whole team ostracized me the whole way back on the train. It was pretty funny, in a way.

> J.D. Salinger, *The Catcher in the Rye*, 1951

Naïfs don't get it, either because they are a child, or are immature, or are in some way limited by factors that hinder comprehension and expression. For Salinger's protagonist Holden Caulfield, the incident above was far from 'funny', but as a machismo teenager he still refuses to acknowledge his upset and tries to breeze through it. Throughout the book, he pretends to understand the world while his actions belie this bravado.

One of the most famous modern examples of a naïf narrator is Forrest Gump from the eponymous 1994 film. Forrest takes us through the film, but comedy and tragedy lie in his continuous miscomprehension of events.

The great strength of this narrative device lies in the trust it places in the recipient—there is nuance and implication, but explicit truths are left for us to interpret. This creates engaging work that requires us to interact on a deeper and more profound level. Here is Mark Haddon's autistic narrator in his 2003 novel *The Curious Incident of the Dog in the Night-time*:

> He said, 'I have spoken to your father and he says that you didn't mean to hit the policeman.'
> I didn't say anything because this wasn't a question.
> He said, 'Did you mean to hit the policeman?'.
> I said, 'Yes.'
> He squeezed his face and said, 'But you didn't meant to hurt the policeman?'.
> I thought about this and said, 'No. I didn't meant to hurt the policeman. I just wanted him to stop touching me.'
> Then he said, 'You know that it is wrong to hit a policeman, don't you?'.
> I said, 'I do.'
> He was quiet for a few seconds, then he asked, 'Did you kill the dog, Christopher?'.
> I said, 'I didn't kill the dog.'

POLYPHONY
seeing it from all angles

POLYPHONY is the interweaving of musical parts (or voices) to create a unified whole. POLYPHONIC NARRATIVES feature different speakers and voices, who offer contrasting perspectives on events to move a story forward. Russian scholar Mikhail Bakhtin [1895-1975] held up the works of Fyodor Dostoevsky as an example. A polyphonic work displays a dialogic, heteroglossic (multi-tongued) approach to narrative, as opposed to the typically monoglossic (single voiced) approach. This forms

> *a novel in which a variety of conflicting ideological positions are given a voice and set in play both between and within individual speaking subjects, without being placed and judged by an authoritative authorial voice.* David Lodge, The Art of Fiction, 2011

Whereas 19th century novels used polyphonic approaches to span great personal or geographical distances to create dramatic irony (e.g. Jonathan Harker's *Transylvania* or Mina Harker's *London*), 21st century writers instead use polyphony to explore histories from multiple perspectives *without* single voice judgements or answers. Here is Nigerian writer Chimamanda Ngozi Adichie on the problem of monoglossic literature:

> *It is impossible to talk about the single story without talking about power. There is a word, an Igbo word, that I think about whenever I think about the power structures of the world, and it is "nkali." It's a noun that loosely translates to "to be greater than another." Like our economic and political worlds, stories too are defined by the principle of nkali. How they are told, who tells them, when they're told, how many stories are told, are really dependent on power.* TED talk: The Danger of a Single Story

In her 2006 novel *Half of a Yellow Sun*, Adichie focalises the perspectives of three very different characters, weaving them together to capture the experience of the 1967 Biafran war in Nigeria. Traversing age, race and class, we see the war through eyes of the poor houseboy Ugwu, the privileged and beautiful Olanna, and the British writer Richard.

Whether in first-person central, third-person focalised, or both, there are no limits to how deep or creative one can go with polyphony. On page 15 we saw the eight narrators of *A Game of Thrones*. On page 21 we met the two narrators of *Gone Girl*. Bram Stoker's 1897 epistolary novel *Dracula* has no singular narrator or protagonist. Wilkie Collins' 1860 mystery novel *The Woman in White* features multiple narrators, including most of the principal characters. Deborah Levy's 2004 novel *Small Island* features four different narrators: Hortense, Queenie, Gilbert and Bernard, who recount diverse experiences of Jamaican immigration to Britain post World War II in a non linear and shifting narrative.

Recognising that even our individual selves are made up of competing voices, Doris Lessing's *The Golden Notebook* contains extracts from four different notebooks written by the same woman:

> a black notebook, which is to do with Anna Wulf the writer; a red notebook, concerned with politics; a yellow notebook, in which I make stories out of my experience; and a blue notebook which tries to be a diary. Doris Lessing, The Golden Notebook, 1962

As John Mullan writes in his review for this novel:

> The idea of a novel containing multiple narratives is hardly new. What was - and is - extraordinary about The Golden Notebook is the use of multiple narratives that all in some sense belong to the same character.

WHO SEES THE STORY?
focalisation and viewpoint characters

Within any given narrative situation the person who actually 'sees' what is happening is called the **FOCALISER**. The focaliser is who we are following, either from the outside, the inside, or both. The **FOCALISATION**, or *point of view*, shifts the moment the narrator starts to follow another character. This might never happen in an entire book, or it might occur only after 100 pages, or in each new chapter, or even within a few paragraphs.

French literary theorist Gérard Genette [1930-2018] identified two types of focalization: **INTERNAL**, or *intradigetic*, where the narrator has access to the thoughts and feelings of the focaliser, and **EXTERNAL**, or *extradigetic*, where the narrator sees things from the focaliser's point of view, but cannot read their minds. In visual media there is usually no narrator as such, but there is focalisation. In the movie world this is termed **POV** (point of view) and is ultimately controlled by the director, the *de facto* narrator.

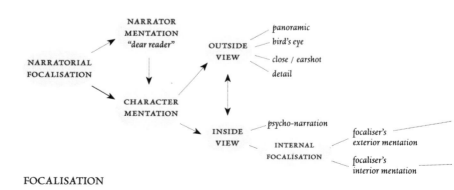

FOCALISATION

N	HETERODIEGETIC	HOMODIEGETIC	HETERODIEGETIC	HETERODIEGETIC
F_1	FIXED EXTERNAL	FIXED INTERNAL	FIXED INTERNAL	DYNAMIC INTERNAL
F_2	NARRATOR	NARRATOR (= CHARACTER)	ONE CHARACTER, NON-NARRATING	MULTIPLE CHARACTERS, NON-NARRATING

She walked into the bar, and he watched her. He stood with some of his friends, but his eyes were across the room with her, as she hung up her coat, greeted a friend, and ordered a drink from a waitress. Eventually, he left his pals and began to cross the floor.	I lost my breath every time she walked into the bar. The sight of her made me feel alive again. I had to say something to her, but I didn't know how. After standing there like a frightened child, I finally excused myself from my friends and went to talk to her.	He watched as she entered the bar, took off her coat and greeted a friend. Her beauty left him breathless. Made him feel alive again. He knew he had to speak to her, but how? It didn't matter. He was tired of feeling like a frightened child. He excused himself and crossed the floor.	As she entered the bar, she wondered if he'd noticed her. She'd worn this dress for him, but she still felt invisible. How could she have known that across the room he pined for her? Like a frightened child he searched his mind for some excuse to speak with her. How could she have known that she took his breath away and made him feel alive again? At last, she saw him making his way across the bar towards her. Her heart began to race.

ABOVE: *A scene written in four different focalisations.* N=Narrator. F_1=Focalisation, F_2=Focaliser.
FACING PAGE: *The Framework of Focalisation, showing the various options open to an author.*
BELOW: *The Processes of Mentation, a little window on to the mind.* (Diagrams after Manfred Jahn).

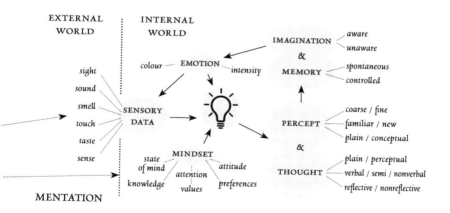

DISTANCE
in deep or far out

An omniscient narrator can describe anything, from any viewpoint, and any distance. Something can be described from afar, observed across a room, experienced close up, or lived inside someone's head. Writers carefully control these distances, moving between them as the situation requires.

> *A novel's narrative takes the reader inside one or more characters, to evoke thoughts, feelings, perceptions and moment-by-moment physical experience. Crucially, this isn't a binary inside/outside decision, it's a spectrum, with the writer controlling how deep we feel we are inside that subjective, individual, close-up of a character's consciousness. And the writer also controls how far out the narrative takes us, towards an objective, wide-angle telling of those events that is beyond any one character's experience.* Emma Darwin

There are three kinds of narrative distance, with five distances each:

NARRATOR DISTANCE: The degree of personal connection between the narrator and the reader in any narrative:

1. **REMOTE:** *It was a dark and stormy night.*
2. **NEAR:** *Our tale begins with a sudden flash of lightning.*
3. **CLOSE:** *Did you enjoy thunderstorms as a child, reader, or did they scare you?*
4. **INTIMATE:** *I have always loved flashes and bangs.*
5. **PARTICIPATORY:** *That night, the sky exploded around me.*

PHYSICAL DISTANCE: The exterior space between the narrator and the event or character they are describing:

1. **REMOTE:** *The rain lashed across the valley.*
2. **NEAR:** *They were safe under the greak oak.*
3. **CLOSE:** *"We could run for it", he said.*

4. **INTIMATE:** *She smiled.*

5: **PARTICIPATORY:** *Tiny raindrops flecked her cheeks.*

PSYCHIC DISTANCE: The interior space between the narrator and the thoughts and feelings of other characters in the narrative:

1. **REMOTE:** *It was winter of the year 1853. A large man stepped out of a doorway.*

2. **NEAR:** *Henry J. Warburton had never much cared for snowstorms.*

3. **CLOSE:** *Henry hated snowstorms.*

4. **INTIMATE:** *God how he hated these damn snowstorms.*

5. **PARTICIPATORY:** *Snow. Under your collar, down inside your shoes, freezing and plugging up your miserable soul.* John Gardner, The Art of Fiction, 1983

Remote distances are good for setting a scene; closer ones suit intensity and subjectivity. Narrative coach Rachel Smith uses this example, from Kate Morton's 2012 novel *The Secret Keeper*, to demonstrate variable distance:

> *A clutch of hens appears from nowhere to peck between the bricks of the garden patch, a jay drags his shadow across the garden, a tractor in the nearby meadow putters to life. And high above it all, lying on her back on the floor of a wooden tree house, a girl of sixteen pushes the lemon Spangle she's been sucking hard against the roof of her mouth and sighs.*
>
> *It was cruel, she supposed, just to let them keep hunting for her, but with the heatwave and the secret she was nursing, the effort of games — childish games at that — was just too much to muster. Besides, it was all part of the challenge and, as Daddy was always saying, fair was fair and they'd never learn if they didn't try.*

WHEN IS THE STORY TOLD?
tense and aspect

The **TENSE** of a narrative indicates when it happened. Choosing the appropriate tense for your writing is an important decision. Most narratives are set either in the **PAST** (and are **RETROSPECTIVE**) or unfold in the **PRESENT** (so are **CURRENT**). Occasionally, they are predictive of **FUTURE** events (and are **ANTICIPATORY**). They can also be a mixture of all three.

In English, there are four primary **ASPECTS** to each of the three tenses (other languages can have more). These indicate how the event occurs in time, in particular whether it is ongoing or complete (*see table opposite*). Although some of these are impractical for literary purposes, each creates a slightly different pace and tone, and characterises the narrator in a slightly different way. If you are writing a book, try writing the same scene in various different tenses to see which best suits your story.

Past tense is by far the most common narrative form—the classic way to tell a story. It is, however, rare to stay in past tense throughout an entire novel, so, depending on the particular moment an author is describing, they often flit between aspects. For example, *She talked to her neighbour* is **SIMPLE PAST** tense, effectively the 'now' of the narrative; however, to describe another conversation that took place prior to this will require a shift to the **PAST PERFECT**: *she had talked to her other neighbour*. The extract below is an example of coherent aspect switching:

> *The first time I laid eyes on Terry Lennox he was drunk in a Rolls-Royce Silver Wraith outside the terrace of The Dancers. The parking lot attendant had brought the car out and he was still holding the door open because Terry Lennox's left foot was still dangling outside, as if he had forgotten he had one.*

Raymond Chandler, *The Long Goodbye*, 1953

TENSE

		PAST	PRESENT	FUTURE
ASPECT	SIMPLE:	It began and ended in the past: I SHOWERED and the doorbell rang	It begins and ends in the present: I SHOWER and the doorbell rings	It will begin and end in the future: I WILL SHOWER and the doorbell will ring
	CONTINUOUS:	It was ongoing in the past: I WAS SHOWERING when the doorbell started ringing	It is ongoing in the present: I AM SHOWERING when the doorbell rings	Ongoing in the future: I WILL BE SHOWERING when the doorbell rings
	PERFECT:	It completed in the past: I HAD SHOWERED when the doorbell rang	It is completed in the present: I HAVE SHOWERED when the doorbell rings	It will be completed: I WILL HAVE SHOWERED when the doorbell rings
	PERFECT CONTINUOUS:	It had been ongoing: I HAD BEEN SHOWERING when the doorbell rang	Is has been ongoing: I HAVE BEEN SHOWERING when the doorbell rings	It will be ongoing: I WILL HAVE BEEN SHOWERING when ...

ABOVE: The three tenses and four aspects of modern English. Tense conveys <u>when</u> an event occurs in time. Aspect conveys <u>how</u> an event occurs in time.

The HABITUAL aspect is also useful. This indicates an action which occurs regularly or repeatedly: She would talk to her neighbour every day, or I can talk to my neighbour for hours. It can build background and context.

The exploration of time in literature continues to evolve. Audrey Niffenegger's 2003 bestseller *The Time Traveler's Wife* uses present tense narration as part of the fabric of meaning in the novel. The narrator is forced to live in a present in which her husband Henry is flung about in time throughout the chronology of their lives together:

I am speechless. Here is Henry, calm, clothed, younger than I have ever seen him. Henry is working at the Newberry Library, standing in front of me, in the present. Here and now. I am jubilant. Henry is looking at me patiently, uncertain but polite.

PAST TENSE
it was raining

The **PAST TENSE** remains the most popular choice for fiction. Readers today are so used to it that they often forget about it being in the past and experience the narrative as though it is unfolding right before them in the present. The use of present tense in dialogue adds to the illusion:

> ...Lucy was so excited that they all went back with her into the room. She rushed ahead of them, flung open the door of the wardrobe and cried, "Now! go in and see for yourselves."
>
> "Why, you goose," said Susan, putting her head inside and pulling the fur coats apart, "it's just an ordinary wardrobe; look! there's the back of it."
>
> Then everyone looked in and pulled the coats apart; and they all saw— Lucy herself saw— a perfectly ordinary wardrobe. There was no wood and no snow, only the back of the wardrobe, with hooks on it. C. S. Lewis, The Lion, the Witch and the Wardrobe, 1950

Past tense, with its stamp of time-tested respectability, is also considered easier to write than present tense. Stories told in the past tense are highly flexible: since the events are in the past, the narrator can relate them in whatever order best suits their scheme. The past tense also allows the use of techniques like foreshadowing to create tension:

> The Doctor found him extremely quick to learn and within a few weeks Steerpike was in control of all the dispensary work. Indeed, the chemicals and drugs had a strong fascination for the youth and he would often be found compiling mixtures of his own invention.
>
> Of the compromising and tragic circumstances that were the outcome of all this, is not yet time to speak. Mervyn Peake, Gormenghast, 1950

Peake's use of the continuous habitual 'would often be found compiling' adds to the sense of present danger.

PRESENT TENSE

the sun is shining

The increasingly common use of **PRESENT TENSE** was catalysed by Charlotte Perkins Gilman's 1892 short story *The Yellow Wallpaper*, where its use perfectly captures her narrator's slow descent into insanity:

> We have been here two weeks, and I haven't felt like writing before, since that first day. I am sitting by the window now, up in this atrocious nursery, and there is nothing to hinder my writing as much as I please, save lack of strength.

In present tense, the reader rolls with the punches in a here-and-now narrative full of immediacy and detail:

> Boys are playing basketball around a telephone pole with a backboard bolted to it. Legs, shouts. The scrape and snap of Keds on loose alley pebbles seems to catapult their voices high into the moist March air blue above the wires. Rabbit Angstrom, coming up the alley in a business suit, stops and watches, though he's twenty-six and six three. So tall, he seems an unlikely rabbit, but the breadth of white face, the pallor of his blue irises, and a nervous flutter under his brief nose as he stabs a cigarette into his mouth partially explain the nickname, which was given to him when he too was a boy. He stands there thinking, the kids keep coming, they keep crowding you up.

John Updike, *Rabbit, Run*. 1960

Present tense, with its ever-advancing unfolding single moment, forces the reader to stay close to the focalised character. It can be tricky to use with multiple focalisers, but when combined with a first person narrator it can transport a reader right into someone else's experience, something that the written word still does better than any other medium.

Present tense is ideal for shorter novels, short stories, flashbacks, and the occasional focalised experience of a particular viewpoint character.

FUTURE TENSE
it will shine again

Future tense relies on the use of modal verbs, such as *will, shall, may, might, could,* plus auxilliary verbs, such as *am, are, is, be,* and temporal adverbs, such as *soon, always, before, lately.* So, for example. the present tense phrase *He is running* can be transformed into the future tense by adding an auxiliary verb, *He will be running,* or by adding an adverb, *He is running tomorrow.*

Future tense is uncommon in the written word, but when used effectively can be a powerful device. The extract below from the opening of Jane Austen's 1817 *Northanger Abbey* is a prime example:

> But when a young lady is to be a heroine, the perverseness of forty surrounding families cannot prevent her. Something must and will happen to throw a hero in her way.

Austen's novel is a gentle parody of Gothic fiction and her use of future tense anticipates the tropes of this form, adding to the wry humour.

Future tense appears in ancient prophecies and in poems. It is also used in thrillers, when a character is worrying (*see page 55*), and in movies, either when the protagonist outlines their plan to save the day:

> DOC BROWN: *At the calculated moment, you'll take off from down the street, driving right toward the cable, accelerating to 88. Lightning will strike the clock tower, electrifying the cable, just as the car's connecting hook makes contact, thereby sending 1.21 jigowatts into the flux capacitor and sending you back to 1985.* Back to the Future, 1985

or when the antagonist(s) reveals their dastardly plan(s):

> MOLA RAM: *They dig for the gems to support our cause. They also search for the last two stones. Soon we will have all five Sankara Stones and the Thuggees will be all powerful.* Gloria Katz & Willard Huyck, Indiana Jones and the Temple of Doom, 1984

MIXED TENSES
it will be as it was

Some authors change tenses midway through a book. The first two thirds of Mervyn Peake's 1946 novel *Titus Groan* are written in past tense, the last third in present tense. Other authors repeatedly seesaw between the present and past, albeit with careful attention to the chronology of their stories, chapter by chapter, or even phrase by phrase, as here:

> *Is that how we lived, then? But we lived as usual. Everyone does, most of the time. Whatever is going on is as usual. Even this is as usual, now.*
> *We lived, as usual, by ignoring. Ignoring isn't the same as ignorance, you have to work at it.* Margaret Atwood, *The Handmaid's Tale*, 1985

The ability to move between different tenses is part of any good writer's toolkit. Handled in a consistent manner, these shifts can feel very natural in the narrative; or they can deliberately jar for dramatic effect:

> *Mrs Dalloway said she would buy the flowers herself. For Lucy had her work cut out for her. The doors would be taken off their hinges. Rumpelmayer's men were coming. And then, thought Clarissa Dalloway, what a morning — fresh as if issued to children on a beach. What a lark!* Virginia Woolf, *Mrs Dalloway*, 1925

Angela Carter is another master of tense manipulation:

> *That was the way I walked into the bird-haunted solitude of the Erl-King ... Goat's milk to drink, from a chipped tin mug; we shall eat the oatcakes he has baked on the hearthstone. Rattle of the rain on the roof.* Angela Carter, *The Erl-King*, 1979

These examples open in sturdy past tense, before bounding between present, past and future—even changing tense mid sentence—alluding to the effect of the past upon the present and future, and vice versa.

HOW IS THE STORY TOLD?
narrative structure

There are five basic types of narrative structure:

1. **LINEAR / CHRONOLOGICAL.** *Most of the story is told in the order in which it occurs. There may be occasional temporal discontinuities, such as flashbacks, but the narrative essentially progresses chronologically. The most common structure.*

2. **CYCLIC.** *The story begins where it ends, often near the chronological end of the story, which may then carry on for a while afterwards (see below).*

3. **NONLINEAR / FRACTURED.** *The story is told out of chronological order, and may even jump disjointedly around the timeline (see opposite).*

4. **PARALLEL.** *The story follows multiple storylines and characters, unified by a theme, event, mission or character (see page 34).*

5. **INTERACTIVE.** *The reader makes choices throughout, leading to different scenes and alternative endings. Difficult in literary form, but common in video games.*

A **CYCLIC** or **CIRCULAR NARRATIVE** begins and ends in the same place. The story may open *in media res* (in the middle of the action), or near the chronological end of the tale, before going back over the events that led up to this point. Cyclic narratives can hook a reader right from the start with the power of the final unresolved climax, a situation which also comes with plenty of dramatic irony, as we know what is going to happen (just not how, or why) while the characters know nothing.

Danny Boyle's 2009 film *Slumdog Millionaire* is a cyclic narrative. It opens with the lead character, Jamal, starring on an Indian television quiz show, one question away from the 20 million rupee prize. Suddenly, he is detained by the police, who cannot believe Jamal is not cheating. Then, through a series of flashbacks, we learn how Jamal knew each answer, from events in his life. The police inspector believes him, as the movie catches up to the beginning and then continues, concluding with him correctly guessing the final answer and reuniting with his love.

S. E. Hinton's 1967 novel *The Outsiders* has a circular structure. Right at the end of the book, deciding to share his own difficult story in his essay for English class, impulsive 14-year-old Ponyboy writes the same words that we read at the beginning—the story of being jumped by the upper-class Socs after leaving a movie. He hasn't really moved on.

A NONLINEAR or FRACTURED NARRATIVE portrays events out of chronological order. It is often used to mimic the inner life of a character. In *The Life and Opinions of Tristram Shandy* by Laurence Sterne, published in nine volumes from 1759 to 1767, the eponymous narrator tells his life story. Tristram's repeated digressions and diversions, along with his chaotic chronological arrangment of the events in his life, contribute to a fractured narrative which almost resembles a stream of consciousness.

Joseph Heller's satirical war novel *Catch-22*, published in 1953, uses non-chronological third-person omniscient narration, describing events from different characters' POV.

Orson Welles uses non-chronological flashback to tell the story of his protagonist in the 1941 film *Citizen Kane*, and Akira Kurosawa uses it to show conflicting versions of the same story in his 1950 film *Rashomon*.

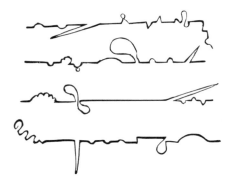

ABOVE: *Nonlinear plot lines, illustration from Laurence Sterne's* The Life and Opinions of Tristram Shandy, *1759-67*

PARALLEL NARRATIVES
structures alongside structures

PARALLEL NARRATIVES feature multiple narrative perspectives which initially seem unconnected but are eventually drawn together, or revealed to be entwined. Writer Linda Aronson identifies six types:

1. **TANDEM.** *Equally-weighted stories running simultaneously. Often didactic and community-wide in theme. Held together by a macro plot or some other device.*

2. **CONSECUTIVE.** *Equally-weighted self-contained stories, told sequentially then connected at the end. Can involve different perspectives / fractured narrative.*

3. **DOUBLE JOURNEY.** *Two central characters, journeying towards, apart or parallel to each other, physically, emotionally or both, each with their own plotlines.*

4. **MULTIPLE PROTAGONIST.** *A group of lead characters. Stories about friendship groups, reunions, families, missions. All protagonists are windows on to the theme.*

5. **FLASHBACK.** *Nine types: Illustration, Regret, Bookend, Catch-up, Preview, Slo-mo, Thwarted Dream, Case History, Autobiographical.*

6. **FRACTURED.** *Parallel stories, often in different time-frames, fractured, truncated and remixed to reveal unexpected connections and consequences.*

Philip Henscher explains his decision to use the parallel technique in his 2014 novel *The Emperor Waltz*:

> I wanted to find a way of writing a novel that showed how people at very different times dealt with similar circumstances in similar ways… In the end, I think we're connected by more than we understand, and the novel can explain some of that shared humanity by placing quite unconnected events side by side.

In parallel narratives, although they may cross and join, characters and their stories exist in their own worlds and follow their own narrative arcs.

This differs from a multiple narrator narrative, which presents the same story arc in a broadly chronological order (e.g. *Wuthering Heights*).

Contemporary author David Mitchell has embraced the style. In his 1999 novel *Ghostwritten*, each chapter is a discrete story with a separate protagonist, connected by seemingly minor events. In *Cloud Atlas*, 2004, Mitchell nests six stories, each recounted by a lead character in the next, and each interrupted at a key moment, until the the self-contained sixth story, after which the earlier stories are then concluded. Most of the main characters are reincarnations of each other, each learning and growing, connecting the past to the future, through the parallel narratives.

Haruki Murakami is another master of the art. His 2009 novel *1Q84* follows a promiscuous assassin, Masami Aomame, in a strangely altered version of the year 1984, alongside her childhood classmate, maths teacher Tengo Kawana, who is living in the unaltered version of 1984. The complex parallel plot strands eventually form an intricate web.

In Quentin Tarantino's 1994 movie *Pulp Fiction*, we meet a range of characters with completely different narrative arcs, but all connected to one character, crime boss Marcellus Wallace (played by Ving Rhamyes).

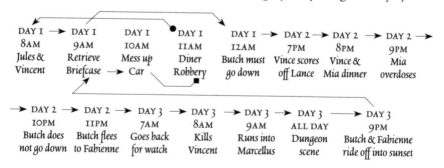

ABOVE: The cyclic timeline for Pulp Fiction. Start at the black dot to follow the ordering in the movie.

FRAMING
and she told me this story

FRAMING describes how stories are presented, or contextualised. Some stories are told straight up; others are framed within another story. Sylvia Plath dives, frameless, straight into her semi-autobiographical novel:

> *It was a queer, sultry summer, the summer they electrocuted the Rosenbergs, and I didn't know what I was doing in New York.* Sylvia Plath, The Bell Jar, 1963

Frames can entice a reader more gradually into a storyworld, while adding a gloss of authenticity. The technique is as old as storytelling itself. Ancient Egyptian examples, written on papyrus c.1850 BC, include *The Eloquent Peasant* and *The Tale of the Shipwrecked Sailor*, summarised here:

> *A sailor returning from a failed voyage at sea, is anxious about how the king will receive him. To reassure him, an attendant tells him a story of his own, of a voyage in which he overcame disaster, including meeting with a god and the king.*

Similar **FRAMING DEVICES** are used in the ancient Indian *Mahābhārata*, compiled c.400 BC. This epic is initially recited by the sage Vaiśampāyana to King Janamejaya, the great-grandson of prince Arjuna. The story is then recited again, many years later, by storyteller Ugraśrava to a group of sages attending King Saunaka Kulapati in the Naimiśa Forest.

Framing is used by Homer in his epic *Odyssey*, c.800 BC, when Odysseus suddenly becomes the first-person narrator in the middle of the tale:

BOOKS 1-4: *Exposition. We learn that Odysseus has not returned and is missing.*
BOOKS 5-8: *Escape. We find Odysseus captive on an island. He escapes.*
| **BOOKS 9-12**: *Tales. "I, Odysseus, now tell you, Phaeacians, my adventures."*
BOOKS 13-20: *Return. We follow as Odysseus he returns home.*
BOOKS 21-24: *Climax. Odysseus slays the suitors.*

FRAME NARRATIVES can set the scene for a multitude of other stories. Giovanni Boccaccio's 1352 *Decameron* contains 100 stories from 10 narrators, waiting out the plague in a country house near Florence. In *The Canterbury Tales*, c.1390, our writer/narrator Geoffrey Chaucer is embarking on a pilgrimage to Canterbury when he meets 29 fellow travellers at a tavern outside London. They agree to travel together and compete to tell stories (24 in all) to make the journey pass quicker and win a free meal:

That ech of yow, to shorte with oure weye / In this viage shal telle tales tweye [....]
And which of yow that bereth hym best of alle / That is to seyn, that telleth in this caas /
Tales of best sentence and moost solaas / Shal have a soper at oure aller cost

Shakespeare uses a framing device in *Hamlet*, when in Act 3 Scene 2, Hamlet encourages a group of players to enact a play, *The Murder of Gonzago*. In this play within a play, the contrived murder scene prompts the watching murderer Claudius to flee the room, signifying his guilt.

First-personal peripheral narration is a form of framing, and a first-person central narrator can tell stories, even quite long ones, within their primary narrative. Washington Irvine's early 19th Century *Sketch Book* is framed within the experiences of fictional narrator Geoffrey Crayon. It contains essays on subjects as diverse as rural life in the English countryside to the celebration of Christmas, as well as folk stories that have since leapt right out of the frame to become famous in their own right, such as *The Legend of Sleepy Hollow* and *Rip Van Winkle*.

ABOVE: *Early woodcut for* The Canterbury Tales

37

CHINESE BOXES
frames within frames

A CHINESE BOX narrative, also known as an EMBEDDED or RUSSIAN DOLL narrative, involves multiple nested frames. A narrator or character on the periphery of the action may introduce us to another character (or more) who then recounts something told to them by someone else, and so on. Step by step these levels later reverse back out to the first frame again.

Mary Shelley's 1818 *Frankenstein* is a Chinese Box with three first-person narrators. We begin with four letters from trustworthy Captain Walton:

> CAPTAIN WALTON: *Dear Sister, dear Diary. News! I met this strange man who:*
>> VICTOR FRANKENSTEIN: *Hear this tale. I created a humanoid, who:*
>>> THE CREATURE: *Alas, this is my story. I awoke and…*
>> VICTOR FRANKENSTEIN: *So, you see, a sorry story it is… I continue.*
> CAPTAIN WALTON: *And that is when I met him. This is how it ended.*

If such a fantastical account were told to us directly, we might find it hard to swallow. Instead, Shelley's cleverly embedded narrative structure leads us gently there and back again.

Emily Brontë's 1847 *Wuthering Heights* likewise begins with a relatable narrator, Mr Lockwood, who is staying in the country:

> LOCKWOOD: *Country! Neighbour Heathcliff's odd. I'll ask my housekeeper, Nelly:*
>> NELLY DEAN: *I know all about that family. Here's the story. I remember:*
>>> CATHY: *Nelly, This is my version of events.*
>>> ZILLAH: *This is what happened.*
>>> ISABELLA: *I need to tell you.*
>>> HEATHCLIFF: *I remember it well.*
>> NELLY DEAN: *And that pretty much brings us up to date … a sad story.*
> LOCKWOOD: *A few months later I went back to see their graves. Finis.*

Bronte's use of the nested box structure is particularly skillful, and she gives each narrator a distinctive voice to separate their narratives.

In *The Tale of the Four Dervishes*, written in Persian by Amir Khusro c.1220, a king, depressed by the discovery of his first grey hair, goes wandering in disguise, before coming across four dervishes in a cemetery, who have only just themselves met:

NARRATOR: *Our story follows King Azad Bhakt, who meets four dervishes.*
> TALE OF 1ST DERVISH: *I once fell in love with a mysterious woman.*
>> THE WOMAN'S STORY: *I am the Princess of Damascus. My story …*
> TALE OF 2ND DERVISH: *I am the Prince of Persia. A wise man told me:*
>> THE STORY OF HATIM TAI: *A lesson in generosity.*
> 2ND DERVISH RESUMES: *I also met a princess, and a strange man …*
>> THE STRANGE MAN'S STORY: *I am the Prince of Nimroz, etc.*
> AZAD BHAKT TELLS HIS STORY: *I am actually King Azad Bhakt, etc.*
> TALE OF 3RD DERVISH: *I was born a Prince of Persia. I met an old man.*
>> THE OLD MAN'S STORY: *I am Niman Saiyah, etc.*
> TALE OF 4TH DERVISH: *I am a Prince of China. My story involves a beggar:*
>> THE BEGGAR'S STORY: *I come from a celebrated family, etc.*
NARRATOR: *And King Azag Bhakt had a son, and fixed everything.*

A Chinese Box for children is Julia Donaldson's bestselling 2005 book *Charlie Cook and his Favourite Book*, illustrated by Axel Scheffler:

Once upon a time there was a boy called Charlie Cook
Who curled up in a cosy chair and read his favourite book …
> *About a leaky pirate ship which very nearly sank*
> *And a pirate chief who got the blame and had to walk the plank.*
> *The chief swam to an island and went digging with his hook.*
> *At last he found a treasure chest and in it was a book …*
>> *About a girl called Goldilocks… etc. etc. and Baby Bear said "Look!"*
>> *She's in my bed, and what is more, she's got my favourite book …*
>>> *About Sir Percy Pilkington … etc. etc.…*

LETTERS & OTHER OBJECTS
hooks for hanging frames

A fashion in 18th and 19th century novels was to frame a narrative using artefacts. EPISTOLARY NARRATIVES use letters, diary entries, newspaper clippings and telegrams to aid the suspension of disbelief and provide multiple viewpoints. Modern equivalents use emails, text messages, etc.

Samuel Richardson's 1748 novel *Clarissa* unfolds through the letters of innocent virginal Clarissa Harlowe and seducer Robert Lovelace. Some 537 letters make up the narrative, building tension with dramatic irony, as both characters know something the other doesn't, while we, reading between the lines, understand even more, except for what happens next.

Wilkie Collins' 1859 bestseller *The Woman in White* opens with:

CONTENTS
The First Epoch
  THE STORY BEGUN BY WALTER HARTRIGHT (*account*)
  THE STORY CONTINUED BY VINCENT GILMORE (*letter*)
  THE STORY CONTINUED BY MARIAN HALCOMBE (*diary entry*)
The Second Epoch
  THE STORY CONTINUED BY MARIAN HALCOMBE (*diary entry*)
  THE STORY CONTINUED BY FREDERICK FAIRLIE Esq (*account*)
  etc ... (parenthesis added)

At the beginning of Henry James' 1898 novella *The Turn of the Screw*, our attention is drawn to the character of Douglas, who is in possession of a letter which turns out to contain a most terrifying tale:

Is in old, faded ink, and in the most beautiful hand ... A woman's. She has been dead these twenty years. She sent me the pages in question before she died.

FOUND OBJECT NARRATIVES are framed within artefacts that have been discovered somewhere exotic or romantic, and then revealed to the world. Count Jan Potocki's 1805 novel *The Manuscript Found in Saragossa* is an eponymous example. The technique once again widens distance between the narrative and the reader, helping suspend disbelief in the narrative, and making it feel as if some great hidden secret is being revealed. Many early Gothic novels, such as Horace Walpole's 1764 novel *The Castle of Otranto*, used it to separate the writer from the content. This protected the author's reputation, as Gothic was initially seen as an embarrassing genre to be affiliated with—silly literature for flighty young women. This is why Walpole opens his novel with an entirely false preface:

The following work was found in the library of an ancient Catholic family in the north of England. It was printed at Naples, in the black letter, in the year 1529. How much sooner it was written does not appear. The principal incidents are such as were believed in the darkest ages of Christianity; but the language and conduct have nothing that savours of barbarism. The style is the purest Italian.

More recently, the notorious 1999 movie *The Blair Witch Project* presents the film as if it were found a year after the disappearance of those who feature in it. Viewers are greeted with the following message:

In October of 1994, three student filmmakers disappeared in the woods near Burkittsville, Maryland while shooting a documentary called "The Blair Witch Project". A year later their footage was found.

INVENTING TRUTH
fiction masquerading as fact

One mischievous technique to encourage suspension of disbelief involves creating authoritative sources that legitimise a fictional account.

At the end of Ian McEwan's novel *Enduring Love* there is an appendix purporting to be an article from the *British Review of Psychiatry*. It details a 'real life' case of De Clérambault's Syndrome, the same disorder that the obsessive antagonist is diagnosed with in the novel. The book received much praise, including for McEwan's *formidably intelligent study of one form of mental illness*—but also some criticism. One reviewer complained that he *simply stuck too close to the facts and failed to allow his imagination to invent*. In fact, the article was penned by Doctors 'Wenn' and 'Camia' (an anagram of 'Ian McEwan'), and two years later McEwan confessed:

> I can confirm that Appendix I of Enduring Love is fictional, based on the novel that precedes it rather than the other way around...

Fake bibliographies and pseudo-academic footnotes are also used. Susannah Clarke constructs a complex web of footnotes and explanations that run parallel to her novel about magic in England, which opens:

> A great magician has said of his profession that its practitioners "...must pound and rack their brains to make the least learning go in, but quarrelling always comes very naturally to them," [1] and the York magicians had proved the truth of this for a number of years. Susannah Clake, Jonathan Strange and Mr Norrell, 2004

At the bottom of the page we see the footnote:

[1] The History and Practice of English Magic, by Jonathan Strange, vol. 1, chap. 2, pub. John Murray, London, 1816.

Referencing a work penned by one of the titular characters adds a whole new layer of meta to the text. Clarke's approach (including the addition of genuine references) underpins one of the book's central themes—the conflict between theoretical and practical magic—and allows her to add weight to a sometimes whimsical genre.

There are also frames that present narratives as 'fictional non fiction'. Orsen Welles' 1938 radio 'news broadcast' of an adaption of H.G Wells' novel *The War of the Worlds* is an infamous example. By framing the story as a real live news broadcast, Welles produced a work so convincing that he created mass panic across America and a subsequent media storm (which he dismissed as *feigned fury*). What opens as a genteel orchestral performance is suddenly interrupted by a correspondent who tells the audience:

> PHILLIPS: *Ladies and gentlemen, this is the most terrifying thing I have ever witnessed ... Wait a minute! Someone's crawling out of the hollow top ... It might be a face. It might be ...* (SHOUT OF AWE FROM THE CROWD) *... Good heavens, some-*

> *thing's wriggling out of the shadow like a gray snake. Now it's another one, and another. They look like tentacles to me. There, I can see the thing's body. It's large, large as a bear and it glistens like wet leather. But that face, it ... Ladies and gentlemen, it's indescribable ...*

The same trick is used by the Coen brothers in their 1996 film *Fargo*:

> *This is a true story. The events depicted took place in Minesota in 1987. At the request of the survivors, the names have been changed. Out of respect for the dead, the rest has been told exactly as it occurred.*

ABOVE: Illustration for *War of the Worlds*

MADELEINE MOMENTS
and other transportation devices

A **MADELEINE MOMENT** is a frame device used to transport a narrative into some other realm, time or segment of the tale. It is named after an episode in Proust's magnum opus *In Search of Lost Time* in which the narrator is flung into an involuntary memory by a small madeleine cake soaked in lime blossom tea, a remembrance that constitutes the rest of the novel:

> And soon, mechanically, dispirited after a dreary day with the prospect of a depressing morrow, I raised to my lips a spoonful of the tea in which I had soaked a morsel of the cake. No sooner had the warm liquid mixed with the crumbs touched my palate than a shiver ran through me and I stopped, intent upon the extraordinary thing that was happening to me. An exquisite pleasure had invaded my senses, something isolated, detached, with no suggestion of its origin. And at once the vicissitudes of life had become indifferent to me, its disasters innocuous, its brevity illusory—this new sensation having had the effect, which love has, of filling me with a precious essence; or rather this essence was not in me, it *was* me. Marcel Proust, In Search of Lost Time, Vol. 1, 1913

This clever technique of Proust's harnesses an everyday experience, that of memories and feelings invoked through sensory recollection, via tastes, smells, and sounds:

> The smell of good bread baking, like the sound of lightly flowing water, is indescribable in its evocation of innocence and delight ... M. F. K. Fisher, The Art of Eating, 1954

Transportational frames are used in advertising. A British example is the Bisto advert where the smell of Bisto gravy transports adults back to childhood, eating their mother's Sunday roast dinner. A similarly nostalgic example occurs in the 2007 film *Ratatouille*, where rat chef Remy produces a dish which transports the snooty old food critic right back into his forgotten happy childhood, leading to a glowing review. In his 2003 'food biography' *Toast*, Nigel Slater's lists foods and associated memories:

Oat cookies reminded me of coming home from school; green beans brought back the smell of the farm wehre I was sent to pick them; Turkish Delight reminded me of Christmas ... But the more I ate the more I realized that not every mouthful produced a memory so sweet. A dish of canned raspberries revisited a violent thrashing ...

Sound is another powerful transportation device. In Tennessee Williams's 1947 play *A Streetcar Named Desire*, the music of the 'blue piano' plays as a **PLASTIC THEATRE** device to show the audience that the character of Blanche is experiencing a flashback to her youth. Plastic theatre was developed by Williams to deepen the experience of the audience. It uses props, lights, sound, stage direction, and costume to convey the psychological states of the characters and expand the themes and ideas of the play. It is not intended to be realistic, but symbolic. In the rape scene, Williams' stage directions say that the walls of the flat "have become transparent", symbolising the encroaching outside, real and sordid world.

Less abstract things can also transport us: a hat, dress, waistcoat, medal, pen, key, stone, tree, flower, view, doorway, room, or photograph. For an exercise, focus on a sensory experience and use it as a narrative frame to create a flashback. Conjure up a memory for yourself or a character. As William Faulkner, a prolific user of this device, once observed:

The past is never dead.
It is not even past.

And suddenly the memory returns. The taste was that of the little crumb of madeleine which on Sunday mornings at...

AUTHORIAL INTERJECTIONS
yes reader, I mean you

An **AUTHORIAL INTERJECTION** (or **INTRUSION**) is where the author steps through the voice of the narrator (generally an omniscient narrator) and addresses the reader directly. This can be for editorial purposes, or so the author can venture an opinion (either as a co-observer on the events or characters of the story, or to comment on wider society).

Victor Hugo, irritated with emphasising the stammer of one of his characters, and sensing that the reader might also be annoyed, tells us:

> (We have noticed once for all Toussaint's stammering. Let us be permitted to indicate it no longer. We dislike the musical notation of an infirmity.) Les Misérables, 1862

Mid scene, Anthony Trollope suddenly opines on human nature before relating it to his heroine's character and then returning to his story:

> There are some moments in life in which both men and women feel themselves imperatively called on to make a confidence; in which not to do so requires a disagreeable resolution and also a disagreeable suspicion. There are people of both sexes who never make confidences; who are never tempted by momentary circumstances to disclose their secrets; but such are generally dull, close, unimpassioned spirits, gloomy gnomes, who live in cold dark mines. There was nothing of the gnome about Eleanor; and she therefore resolved to tell Charlotte Stanhope the whole story about Mr. Slope. Barchester Towers, 1857

Another form of interjection is **BREAKING THE FOURTH WALL**. Imagine a stage, where we, the audience, form one of the four walls around it. When characters reach out of their world to acknowledge us in our world, performance and reality become blurred. This is a form of **METAFICTION**— where work recognises and comments on its own construction. At times, times, breaking the fourth wall feels as though the voice of the author is speaking through the characters, using them as ventriloquist's dummies, often for allegorical or satirical ends. One infamous example comes from Charlotte Brontë's novel *Jane Eyre*, where our eponymous character tells us at the end of the final chapter:

> *Reader, I married him.* Jane Eyre, Charlotte Brontë, 1847.

SOLILOQUISING is a form of fourth wall breaking which has a long and rich history. Throughout the works of Shakespeare, characters step out of the action to offer us MONOLOGUES, ASIDES and confessions, generally to create DRAMATIC IRONY:

> *"Look how our partner's rapt."* Banquo's aside when observing Macbeth

In the 1986 movie *Ferris Bueller's Day Off*, Ferris looks straight into the camera and tells us:

> *Life moves pretty fast. If you don't stop and look around once in a while, you could miss it.*

A similar technique is found in modern comedy dramas such as *Malcolm in the Middle*, *Scrubs*, and *The Office*, where characters are interviewed to create TALKING HEADS in a pseudo-documentary format. Phoebe Waller-Bridge's comedy *Fleabag* [2016–2019] by is characterised by an innovative use of fourth wall breaking—the main character Phoebe makes frequent asides to the viewer, as here in one of the final scenes:

> PRIEST: *"I'd really like to be your friend though."*
> FLEABAG: *"I'd like to be your friend, too". (Aside, to camera) "We'll last a week."*
> PRIEST: *"What was that?"*
> FLEABAG: *"What?"*
> PRIEST: *"Where'd you, where'd you just go?"*
> FLEABAG: *"What?"*

The priest is the only character in the show to 'see' Phoebe break the wall!

WHAT MODE IS USED?
exposition and description

Combining the elements we have discussed so far—voice, focaliser, tense and frame—will create a narrative. However, the telling of that narrative is still limited to only a few **NARRATIVE MODES**—the different categories of writing available to a writer. Some writers favour particular modes, while you may prefer to experiment and mix it up. Modes are the narrative equivalent of scenes: after a pacy action sequence in a Bond film, we often find ourselves sipping martinis nonchalantly in a casino. If there is a lot of dialogue, some action will help break it up a little.

There are varying definitions of narrative modes, but in this book we will focus on five:

> 1. **EXPOSITION/SUMMARY**: *Information and context not present in the scene.*
>
> 2. **DESCRIPTION**: *Content derived from senses.*
>
> 3. **ACTION**: *What the characters are doing; what is happening.*
>
> 4. **DIALOGUE**: *The characters' external speech.*
>
> 5. **THOUGHTS**: *The characters' interior monologue.*

EXPOSITION is where the agenda is to introduce key characters and settings, before getting in to the nitty gritty of the story. Exposition helps your readers/audience to get to know your characters, so they can understand their later actions. A man who irritably squashes an insect in the exposition might later explode with road rage, whereas a man who takes great pains to rescue an insect from a spider's web is clearly highly empathetic, which may explain his later decision to help another character. In the following example, Tolkien surrounds Bilbo Baggins with mysterious local gossip, paving the way for 'peculiar' adventures associated with him:

Bilbo was very rich and very peculiar, and had been the wonder of the Shire for sixty years, ever since his remarkable disappearance and unexpected return. The riches he had brought back from his travels had now become a local legend, and it was popularly believed, whatever the old folk might say, that the Hill at Bag End was full of tunnels stuffed with treasure. And if that was not enough for fame, there was also his prolonged vigour to marvel at. Time wore on, but it seemed to have little effect on Mr. Baggins. J. R. R. Tolkien, The Lord of the Rings, 1954

DESCRIPTION mode is dedicated to 'blowing up' small details and often is closely focused on the senses. Narratives which are overly descriptive can quickly become tedious; a good writer, however, knows when to use this mode to immerse the reader in a moment:

A few light taps upon the pane made him turn to the window. It had begun to snow again. He watched sleepily the flakes, silver and dark, falling obliquely against the lamplight.... Yes, the newspapers were right: snow was general all over Ireland. It was falling on every part of the dark central plain, on the treeless hills, falling softly upon the Bog of Allen and, farther westward, softly falling into the dark mutinous Shannon waves. It was falling, too, upon every part of the lonely churchyard on the hill where Michael Furey lay buried. It lay thickly drifted on the crooked crosses and headstones, on the spears of the little gate, on the barren thorns. James Joyce, The Dead, in Dubliners, 1914

ACTION
then what happened

ACTION is the literary mode that shows the reader what is currently happening in the story. It creates forward movement through the plot:

> As soon as she had left for work I went into my study and wrapped the present I was going to give her at the lunch we had planned that day with her godfather, Professor Kale. I gathered all Parry's letters together, arranged them chronologically and fixed them in a clasp folder. I lay on the chaise longue turning the pages slowly from the beginning, looking out for and marking significant passages. These I typed out, with location references in brackets. By the end, I had four sheets of extracts of which I made three copies, placing each in a plastic folder. Ian McEwan, *Enduring Love*, 1997

Note the way that time changes speed in this passage. Literary educator Mary Kole explains the difference between description (or background 'business' as it is known in theatre) and action, using the example of a passage of writing where a character is chopping some vegetables:

> Action in writing means something that has story consequences. Action means that the protagonist either comes into contact with another character or encounters an obstacle or makes an effort to reach a goal or does something in the world of the story that is significant and moves the story forward. Unless they are cutting vegetables for the stew that they will use to poison the king – and this action is the result of a big decision to finally commit treason – then it's business, not action.

Some of the most iconic action sequences involve chases or conflict, sometimes with second-by-second detail:

> I managed to land on my feet in front of the castle, just clear of Leopardon's flaming wreckage. A second after I landed, a shadow spilled over me, and I turned around to see Sorrento's mech blotting out the sky. He raised its massive left foot, preparing to crush me.

I took three running steps and jumped, firing my jet boots in midleap. The thrust threw me clear just as the Mechagodzilla's huge clawed foot slammed down, forming a crater in the spot where I'd stood a second before. The metal beast let out another earsplitting shriek, followed by hollow, booming laughter. Sorrento's laughter.

Ernest Cline, *Ready Player One*, 2011

Action, like description and exposition, can also be conveyed by dialogue. In this extract from her 1937 bestseller, *Death on the Nile*, Agatha Christie describes one of the most important moments of action in the whole book, moving the plot forward entirely via dialogue and inner thought:

Hercule Poirot was just wiping the lather from his freshly shaved face when there was a quick tap on the door, and hard on top of it Colonel Race entered unceremoniously. He closed the door behind him.

He said: 'Your instinct was quite correct. It's happened.'

Poirot straightened up and asked sharply: 'What has happened?'

'Linnet Doyle's dead — shot through the head last night.'

Poirot was silent for a minute, two memories vividly before him — a girl in a garden at Assuan saying in a hard breathless voice: 'I'd like to put my dear little pistol against her head and just press the trigger,' and another more recent memory, the same voice saying: 'One feels one can't go on — the kind of day when something breaks' — and that strange momentary flash of appeal in her eyes.

ABOVE: *Action grabs us and moves us through the plot.*

DIALOGUE
he said she said

DIALOGIC mode depicts a conversation between two or more characters:

> Story time is compressed time. An entire life can be told in the space of just ninety minutes and still somehow feel complete. It's this compression that's the secret of arresting dialogue'. The Science of Storytelling, Will Storr, 2019

Good dialogue is like panning for gold—the writer has to shake out all of the superfluous filler and just keep the valuable nuggets left over. Robert McKee, in his book *Dialogue: The Art of Verbal Action for Page, Stage, and Screen*, writes that dialogue should function to support other narrative modes: exposition, characterisation, and action. So, if your dialogue is not meeting at least one of these, then throw it back in the river.

The pace with which dialogue unfolds is almost the same on the page as it is in the real world. However, it is also often broken up by action beats, short descriptions which relay the speakers' motions, facial expressions, attitudes and internal thoughts, and also by tags, short phrases like *he said, she asked* (the simpler the better). Here is Suzanne Collins:

> My feet move soundlessly across the tiles. I'm only a yard behind him when I say, "You should be getting some sleep."
>
> He starts but doesn't turn. I can see him give his head a slight shake. "I didn't want to miss the party. It's for us, after all."
>
> I come up beside him and lean over the edge of the rail. The wide streets are full of dancing people I squint to make out their tiny figures in more detail. "Are they in costume?"
>
> "Who could tell?" Peeta answers. "With all the crazy clothes they wear here. Couldn't sleep, either?"

"Couldn't turn my mind off," I say.

"Thinking about your family?" he asks.

"No," I admit a bit guiltily. "All I can do is wonder about tomorrow. Which is pointless, of course." Suzanne Collins, *The Hunger Games*, 2008

In the following example from Truman Capote's 1965 novel *In Cold Blood*, the speaker is a teenage girl on the phone to her friend:

"Well. But we're all so happy about Mother—you heard the wonderful news." Then Nancy said, "Listen," and hesitated, as if summoning nerve to make an outrageous remark. "Why do I keep smelling smoke? Honestly, I think I'm losing my mind. I get into the car, I walk into a room, and it's as though somebody had just been there, smoking a cigarette. It isn't Mother, it can't be Kenyon. Kenyon wouldn't dare ..."

This brief exchange builds the characterisation of everyone mentioned. The dialogue is tight but convincing. Capote knows which details are important to establish and takes time to 'blow up' this conversation.

Here are four questions to ask yourself before you write dialogue:

1. Is this dialogue necessary? Does it contribute to characterization and / or action? Does every exchange progress the scene?
2. Do we need to hear the whole exchange? Could we come into the dialogue as conclusions are drawn?
3. What does each character want out of this conversation? There should be something that drives their dialogue forward, whether stated explicitly, hinted implicitly or hidden entirely. What do your characters have on their minds?
4. What's the hierarchy here? Who holds the power and who is in a weaker position? Power is a huge part of conversation and determines who speaks when, who interrupts, who is swearing, who talks the longest, etc.

THOUGHTS

no-one knows

In first person central the reader has access to the narrator's thoughts. **FREE INDIRECT SPEECH (OR FREE INDIRECT DISCOURSE)** allows a writer to reap the benefits of first person insight while staying in a third person narrative. It is often used in conjunction with third person narration, removing the need for direct or indirect speech and dialogue:

> **DIRECT SPEECH** = 'Why is Phoebe wearing yellow shoes?' she asked.
> **INDIRECT SPEECH** = Why was Phoebe wearing yellow shoes? she wondered.
> **FREE INDIRECT SPEECH** = And why on earth was Phoebe wearing yellow shoes?

Jane Austen was a pioneer of the use of free indirect speech. In the extract below, from *Persuasion*, published in 1817, we are inside Captain Frederick Wentworth's head. Dialogue tags, such as *she asked herself* or *she wondered*, have been jettisoned and there is a natural flow to the writing that starts to mimic how thoughts actually arise.

> *He had not forgiven Anne Elliot. She had used him ill, deserted and disappointed him; and worse, she had shewn a feebleness of character in doing so ...*

Mediated through the mind of the author, the technique can negate the need for fussy description about how a character *feels* or what they *think*:

> *He slept less and less. They gave him opium and began morphine injections. But this brought no relief. At first the muffled sense of anguish he experienced in this semiconscious state came as a relief in that it was a new sensation, but then it became as agonizing, if not more so, than the raw pain.* Tolstoy, The Death of Ivan Ilyich, 1886

The brevity of free indirect speech also creates pace, especially in tense situation. It is widely used in thrillers and crime fiction, as here:

> Blomkvist hesitated. Salander was right now his only hope of rescue. What would she think when she came home and found him not there? He had put the photograph of Martin Vanger wearing the padded jacket on the kitchen table. Would she make the connection? Would she sound the alarm? She is not going to call the police. The nightmare was that she would come to Martin Vanger's house and ring the bell, demanding to know where Blomkvist was. Stieg Larsson, The Girl with the Dragon Tattoo, 2005

Larsson creates tension by having his protagonist mentally list the unspoken pitfalls that could lie ahead, sharing his fears about the situation.

As **INTERIOR MONOLOGUE**, it can replace long-winded retrospection:

> (Where was he this morning for instance? Some committee, she never asked what.) But with Peter everything had to be shared; everything gone into. And it was intolerable, and when it came to that scene in the little garden by the fountain, she had to break with him or they would have been destroyed … Virginia Wolf, Mrs Dalloway

Thoughts can also be typeset in italics. *Shall I maybe show an example here?* Italicised thoughts immediately distinguish free indirect speech from other writing. Editor Russell Harper gives the following example:

> "Why do you hate the South?"
> "I dont hate it," Quentin said, quickly, at once, immediately; "I dont hate it," he said. *I dont hate it* he thought, panting in the cold air, the iron New England dark: *I dont. I dont! I dont hate it! I dont hate it!*
> William Faulkner, Absalom, Absalom! 1936

PUTTING IT ALL TOGETHER
some elements of style

You now have all the tools you need to tell your story: options for narrators, focalisations, tenses, frames and narrative modes. How you wield these tools to create your narrative situation is up to you. Whether your book ends up dialogue-heavy, rich in description, or perfectly balanced in all five modes is up to you. How quickly you move between narrative modes and switch character viewpoints is up to you too:

> Art depends heavily on feeling, intuition, taste. It is feeling, not some rule, that tells the abstract painter to put his yellow here and there, not there, and may later tell him that it should have been brown or purple or pea-green. It's feeling that makes the composer break surprisingly from his key, feeling that gives the writer the rhythms of his sentences, the pattern of rise and fall in his episodes, the proportions of alternating elements, so that dialogue goes on only so long before a shift to description or narrative summary or some physical action. The great writer has an instinct for these things. He has, like a great comedian, an infallible sense of timing. And his instinct touches every thread of his fabric, even the murkiest fringes of symbolic structure. He knows when and where to think up and spring surprises, those startling leaps of the imagination that characterize all of the very greatest writing. John Gardner, The Art of Fiction, 1983

There is one thing left to find—your own writing style. Style is what makes writing unique. Your narrative voice, tense, mode and focalisation may be the instruments in your orchestra, but you are the conductor who determines how that piece of music is played. Two writers might deploy the same narrative approaches, but produce works that are entirely different in terms of style. Truly great authors often have a style so distinctive that you can recognise their work through this alone. Take, for example, Oscar Wilde's signature aphoristic delivery and focus on the aesthetic:

Those who find ugly meanings in beautiful things are corrupt without being charming. This is a fault. Those who find beautiful meanings in beautiful things are the cultivated. For these there is hope. Oscar Wilde, The Picture of Dorian Gray, 1890

John Steinbeck can be spotted through his American vernacular, simple syntax and pared back prose:

In the little houses the tenant people sifted their belongings and the belongings of their fathers and of their grandfathers. Picked over their possessions for the journey to the west. The men were ruthless because the past had been spoiled, but the women knew how the past would cry to them in the coming days. The men went into the barns and the sheds. John Steinbeck, The Grapes of Wrath, 1939

Children's writer Julia Donaldson was the best selling author of the decade 2010-2019 in any age group or genre. Her distinctive style utilises humour, rhyme and rhythm to move her third person past tense narrative along and engage her young audience:

A mouse took a stroll through the deep dark wood.
A fox saw the mouse, and the mouse looked good.
"Where are you going to, little brown mouse?
Come and have lunch in my underground house." Julia Donaldson, The Gruffalo, 1999

Style is intertwined with the author's own idiolect (explored further in our sister book, *Character*) and as Gardner suggests, it comes from the writer's instinct. Know the 'rules' of good writing, know good writers, but do not be straightjacketed by or try to emulate them. If a reader wants to read writing in the style of Charles Bukowski, they will read Charles Bukowski; readers come to new writers hoping to hear a tale well told in an engaging and unique way. Experimenting with narrative approaches, using, for example, the exercises on the next page, will help you to work out which approach suits you best and help to develop your own style.

A NARRATIVE EXERCISE
in four parts

In the *Unthology* journal, author Loree Westron recommends this exercise to help writers experiment with voice, tense, distance and perspective:

1. *Writing in the first person, past tense, recount an incident from your childhood, from the perspective of the child you were at the time. Try to get back into the skin of your former self and experience the world as you did then. Remember to use a child's narrative voice.*

2. *Rewrite this incident in first person, present tense — as if the incident is happening at this very moment and you are that child again. Make the reader experience the same sensations, and see the same things your narrator does.*

3. *Describe the incident from your adult perspective. Think about the things you know now about the circumstances connected to this incident, things you weren't aware of at the time. How does the voice alter? Is it less agitated, more understanding, angrier, philosophical?*

4. *Recount the incident using a third person narrator. Your narrator may or may not be part of the action. He/she can be a dispassionate witness, empathise with the protagonist, or be out to stir up trouble. Your choice will change the way you tell the story.*